She Persisted

MAYA LIN

—INSPIRED BY—

She Persisted

by Chelsea Clinton & Alexandra Boiger

·····································

MAYA LIN

·····································

Written by
Grace Lin

Interior illustrations by
Gillian Flint

PHILOMEL

ᒕ *For* ᒪ

the girls who will stick out because
they stick up for what they believe in.

PHILOMEL BOOKS
An imprint of Penguin Random House LLC, New York

First published in the United States of America by Philomel Books,
an imprint of Penguin Random House LLC, 2022

Text copyright © 2022 by Chelsea Clinton
Illustrations copyright © 2022 by Alexandra Boiger

Philomel Books is a registered trademark of Penguin Random House LLC.

Visit us online at penguinrandomhouse.com.

Library of Congress Cataloging-in-Publication Data is available.

Printed in the United States of America

HC ISBN 9780593403006
10 9 8 7 6 5 4 3 2 1
PB ISBN 9780593403020
10 9 8 7 6 5 4 3 2 1

WOR

Edited by Talia Benamy and Jill Santopolo.
Design by Ellice M. Lee.
Text set in LTC Kennerley.

The publisher does not have any control over and does not assume any responsibility for author
or third-party websites or their content.

DEAR READER,

As Sally Ride and Marian Wright Edelman both powerfully said, "You can't be what you can't see." When Sally said that, she meant that it was hard to dream of being an astronaut, like she was, or a doctor or an athlete or anything at all if you didn't see someone like you who already had lived that dream. She especially was talking about seeing women in jobs that historically were held by men.

I wrote the first *She Persisted* and the books that came after it because I wanted young girls—and children of all genders—to see women who worked hard to live their dreams. And I wanted all of us to see examples of persistence in the face of different challenges to help inspire us in our own lives.

I'm so thrilled now to partner with a sisterhood of writers to bring longer, more in-depth versions of these stories of women's persistence and achievement to readers. I hope you enjoy these chapter books as much as I do and find them inspiring and empowering.

And remember: If anyone ever tells you no, if anyone ever says your voice isn't important or your dreams are too big, remember these women. They persisted and so should you.

Warmly,

Chelsea Clinton

She
Persisted

....

She Persisted: WANGARI MAATHAI

She Persisted: WILMA MANKILLER

She Persisted: PATSY MINK

She Persisted: SALLY RIDE

She Persisted: MARGARET CHASE SMITH

She Persisted: SONIA SOTOMAYOR

She Persisted: MARIA TALLCHIEF

She Persisted: DIANA TAURASI

She Persisted: HARRIET TUBMAN

She Persisted: OPRAH WINFREY

She Persisted: MALALA YOUSAFZAI

MAYA LIN

TABLE OF CONTENTS

....

Maya

Maya Lin was born on October 5, 1959, in Athens, Ohio. But her parents hadn't always lived there. They had both escaped from China after a civil war in which the Chinese Communist Party won. Maya's father, Henry Lin, had to leave China because his family had supported the other side in the civil war. It was dangerous for him to stay in China once the war was over, so he left. Maya's mother, Julia, had the opportunity to attend Smith College in the United States. Even though she had to be smuggled out of Shanghai on a boat and face monsoons and pirates, she was determined to go. And she did!

Henry and Julia met and married in the US. They were far away from their native land, but they were determined to build a life together. After their son, Tan, was born, they moved to Athens, Ohio, to teach at Ohio University. Henry, an artist, became a ceramics professor, and Julia would become an English professor. And then Maya was born.

"All the female Lins are very strong, very independent," Henry once said. "All very talented and very determined."

Maya was destined to be no different. Her

middle name, Ying, meant "precious stone," and though her parents did not realize it when they named her, it was a hint at her future.

As a child, Maya didn't think about strength, independence, talent, or determination. She did think about a precious stone, however. Her brother owned a beautiful geode that she admired greatly. Maya would often borrow the geode. Tan, after finding it on her desk, would bring it back to his. The geode went back and forth between the two desks constantly.

But even more than passing the stone back and forth, young Maya spent most of her time watching the world around her.

The Lins' home was set in the hilly woods, far away from other houses. So, Maya watched the nature that surrounded her. She would sit in

silence, watching the animals and noticing how the streams formed ridges in the land.

Maya watched her father too. She spent hours watching him pull and cut clay. She saw the shades of brown and gray on his potter's wheel. She saw the earthen colors in the plates she used for meals.

She saw the simple shapes of the furniture he made that she used every day.

She also saw her mother's love of learning. Julia earned her PhD and Maya watched her study. Books were everywhere.

But there were some things Maya did not see.

Maya didn't see her grandparents, her aunts or her uncles, since they all still lived in China. And even though they tried to send letters, they knew that China's strict government was reading and changing their messages.

Maya also didn't see many other Chinese Americans. Her family was the only Chinese American one in their town. Her parents wanted Tan and Maya to fit in, so they did not teach them Chinese. Because of this, "I thought I was white," Maya said.

When she wasn't watching the world around her, Maya was making things. At home, she made houses and villages out of paper. After school, Maya and Tan would go to their father's studio and use all the materials there. Often, they would throw clay at the clock to cover the time. Their father would get annoyed, but he never made them leave. They knew, even when they were naughty, that they were always welcome at his studio.

The family spent most of their time together, which meant that Tan was Maya's usual companion. They played chess together and fought like siblings do. Maya often tried to impress Tan—sometimes bragging. He, as the older brother, would try to humble her whenever she acted too proud of herself.

In China, the usual tradition was to favor boys over girls. But Maya's parents didn't treat Tan and Maya differently at all. Maya later said that she was "never told I couldn't do something because I was a girl." Her mother was a role model for her. She was a dedicated scholar. She wrote about Chinese woman poets. She wanted people to know and value these women's important works.

And in Maya's family, it wasn't only about what women were allowed to do—it was about men too. Maya's father had not been happy with his own upbringing, which had been very strict. In China, he had not been allowed to make art, but in the United States he could. These experiences caused Maya's parents to give their children a great amount of freedom. Her parents seemed to think, *We're not going to force Tan or Maya to do anything they don't want to do.*

Maya's family home in the woods was filled with art and ideas, and with the spirit of independent thinking. It was a safe, private space for her family, separate from the community of Athens and, in many ways, from the world.

But while Maya was peacefully watching animals, the world outside was troubled. Black people in the US were demanding full civil rights and to be treated fairly. Several of their leaders, including

Reverend Martin Luther King Jr., were killed. The Vietnam War, in which American soldiers were fighting halfway around the world, raged. People who did not believe Americans should be fighting in that war were protesting. But Maya was not really aware of any of this. It was "a very insulated and isolated childhood," Maya said, but it was one full of thought and possibilities.

CHAPTER 2

....

High School

During high school, Maya had a hard time fitting in. Many of the other girls were interested in makeup and boys, and Maya was not. She didn't date or go to football games or go to the prom, and she never joined any clubs or sports teams. Both Maya and Tan ate dinner at home every night with their parents. She was also the smallest kid in her class, and she later said that she felt like people treated her like a baby sister or a China doll.

Maya spent her time studying, wandering the woods, and creating art—everything from macramé to bronze casting! Her father was now dean of fine arts at Ohio University. Maya used the art supplies and equipment there whenever she could. She thought of the university as a playground.

Maya also got good grades. Very good grades!

Math was her favorite subject, but she excelled at all of them. But she didn't get good grades so she could be better than other students or so she could go to a certain college. She didn't think about those things. "I loved getting straight A's, but that was more for me," Maya said.

However, she did get one F—in gym class! Gym was a nightmare for Maya. Being the smallest, she was always the last to be chosen for teams. She detested gym class and didn't get along with the gym teacher.

But that was the exception. In fact, at school, teachers were the people Maya got along with best. She would stay after school with the chemistry teacher, Mrs. Barensfeld. They would have fun doing science experiments. One time, Maya made too much flash powder and it caused an explosion!

Another teacher ran into the room demanding, "What did I just hear?" Both Maya and Mrs. Barensfeld answered that they heard nothing. And they weren't lying. The blast had been so loud that it made them temporarily deaf!

However, these experiences were not enough to help Maya enjoy high school. By senior year she was miserable. She received special permission to stop taking most of her classes at school and take special classes or do projects at the university instead. These were called "independent studies," and Maya did many of them so she would not have to be at her high school.

She was eager to leave Athens. Maya still loved animals and the environment, so she thought she would become a field zoologist—a kind of scientist who studies animals in their outdoor homes. Many of Maya's classmates believed she would go on to work on something related to English, like her mother. Even though Maya created art every day, no one thought Maya would become an artist. Not even Maya herself!

As Maya finished her high school studies, she decided to apply to Yale University, in New Haven, Connecticut. She didn't think she would get in, since no one from her high school had ever been accepted there before. But she decided to try for it anyway, and in the end, she got in!

So, in the fall of 1977, Maya went to Yale. She was excited for her college years to begin.

C H A P T E R   3

....

Yale

At Yale University, Maya flourished. At first, though, it was a bit overwhelming. She later said that she felt like all the students there were much smarter than her.

Thankfully, at Yale, she found friends who loved learning as much as she did. Her professors valued her creativity. For the first time, Maya felt like she fit in.

Except for one thing. Maya did not feel like

she fit with her own cultural heritage. Maya was still uncomfortable thinking of herself as a Chinese American. When she was invited to join the Asian American Society and saw the group of people there who looked like her, Maya felt very self-conscious. In Ohio, no one looked like her, so it was easier for her to forget that she was Asian. She could almost always pretend that she was white. At the Asian American Society meeting, though, she was reminded otherwise. And she did not like it. "I really was in denial about being Chinese American," Maya said. She decided not to be a part of the group.

When Maya first began at Yale, she still thought she was going to be a field zoologist. That changed when she met her science advisor, Dr. Apville. He told her she probably would not like the program they had there. At Yale, they sometimes experimented on animals when they were still alive. Maya was horrified. She quickly decided to change course.

But she was not sure what new course to take. During her first two years at Yale, she took many kinds of classes—from philosophy to photography. In the end, she knew she liked math and art. But she still did not know where that would lead her. Then, one day at the library, she stared up at the ceiling. She saw lines and paint above her and, suddenly, she knew. She would be an architect—someone who designs buildings and other structures.

Maya completely threw herself into the architecture program. She worked on each project until she was satisfied. She often went without sleep to finish. Maya's professors thought she worked in an

unusual way. Instead of drawing on paper, Maya often used modeling clay to develop—a kind of modeling clay—to develop her designs. After watching her father's hands mold clay to make pots, Maya had learned to do the same thing to make architectural designs. She couldn't help it. "I think with my hands," she said.

In Maya's junior year, she went to study in Denmark. While she was there, she saw a large cemetery that was also used as a park. Maya grew curious about how architecture made people interact with the dead. The next year, when Maya returned to Yale, she and some classmates had to choose a senior project topic. Maya remembered the cemetery. They decided that studying how architecture was used when people died would be an interesting topic for them to explore.

And so, it seemed like fate when Maya's classmate saw a notice posted on a bulletin board at school. It announced a contest to design a memorial for the Vietnam War. It was the perfect assignment for each of them to take on to explore their topic. And it was especially perfect for Maya.

·····························

CHAPTER 4

Thinking with Her Hands

The Vietnam War was a civil war in Vietnam, a country in Southeast Asia. During the war, the US sent a lot of Americans to help South Vietnam fight. Many people in the US were unhappy about the war, and there were large protests against it all over the country. In the end, the Communist forces of North Vietnam won. Over three million people were killed, including more than 58,000 Americans.

Because she had been so cut off from the world around her during her childhood, Maya did not know that much about the Vietnam War. Even so, when Maya began to think about the memorial, she decided not to research it. She knew that the way the government made decisions about the war got people upset. Maya didn't want the memorial to be about those decisions.

Instead, Maya thought about memorials, and about the monuments that usually formed them. What was a monument's purpose? What was the purpose of a monument now, for this war, at this time?

In the past, monuments about wars were usually about the leaders. Sometimes they were about a big battle that had been won. But Maya felt that this memorial should be about the people who fought in the war. She felt that this should be a monument that was honest about those who had paid for this war with their lives. At Yale, there was a place that had all the names of students who had been killed in wars. Maya remembered how, during her freshman and sophomore years, stonecutters chiseled in new names—those of students who had died in the Vietnam War. Maya had touched the names on the wall. She had found them very moving. She realized then, as she later said, "the power of a name."

Over Thanksgiving break, Maya went to go see the site where they wanted to build the memorial. When she saw it, Maya told people later on, she immediately "imagined cutting into the earth and polishing its open sides." It would be like the geode she had borrowed from her brother when she was younger. That geode was an unplanned inspiration for her design.

Maya returned to Yale. She was eager to get to work. She couldn't even wait until she was finished eating in the cafeteria. She tried out her first design idea there, using mashed potatoes!

But she quickly moved on from mashed potatoes as her ideas took shape. Her design would slice
open the earth with two walls that would form
a V shape. The walls would have a dark, glossy
surface. The black, shiny stone would have the
name of every American Vietnam War fallen sol-
dier engraved on it. All of them would be listed
in order of their death. The listing of the names
would begin and end where the two walls came
together—what Maya called the apex—to symbol-
ize the completion of the war. People could search
for the names of the ones they had lost. When
they found the names they were looking for, they
would see their own living faces reflected in the
polished surface. The memorial would be like a
meeting place for the living and the dead. It would
be, Maya said, a link "between our world and the

quieter, darker, more peaceful world beyond."

But was it too simple? Maya tried adding more to her design, but nothing else seemed right. Adding more only distracted from what she was trying to do. In the end, Maya realized that her design had to be simple in order to be powerful.

In the meantime, the competition deadline was approaching. Maya's classmates were using the competition guidelines for their school projects, but no one really planned to enter. Except for Maya.

For the competition, entries needed to be drawings, but they could also include a written description. Maya made her drawings with pastels, which made them look like paintings. They were very mysterious looking, and very unusual for architectural drawings. But Maya knew her written statement would be more important. She knew people might think her design was too simple. Her description would be the only way to make sure the judges would understand what she was trying to accomplish.

Maya worked and reworked her essay. Finally, even though she wasn't finished, she had to send in her entry. With her statement handwritten on presentation boards, she rushed her project to the competition in Washington, DC. Her professor gave her a B. After that, Maya thought that was the end of it.

But she was wrong. Because in May 1981, three officers from the Vietnam Veterans Memorial Fund came to see her. Maya had won the competition!

....

CHAPTER 5

Entry #1026

Maya's design had been chosen out of over 1,400 submissions. The entries were submitted with just numbers, no names, so the competition would be fair. The judges could only decide the winner by how good they thought the entry was, not by who did it. There were many different designs—columns, towers, a peace sign, even a giant statue of boots! But the judging panel kept returning to entry #1026. There was something about it that was special. "There's no escape from its power," one of the judges said. They agreed that entry #1026 was the winner.

At the time, most architects were white men, and the judges had expected the winning designer would be someone with a lot of experience. So, they must have been surprised when they saw the creator of entry #1026 was a twenty-one-year-old Chinese American college student. But Maya's surprise was greater. When officers of the Vietnam Veterans Memorial Fund told Maya she had won, she looked at them blankly. "I think my roommate's face showed more emotion than mine," Maya said. She was so shocked that, at first, she couldn't believe it. But, when she finally realized it was true, she was thrilled.

On the day of Maya's college graduation, she

moved to Washington, DC, to help oversee the memorial's construction.

But then the troubles began.

Unfortunately and unfairly, the fact that Maya was a young Asian American woman made some people angry. Some were mad that she was a woman, while almost all the Americans who had died in the war were men. Some were mad that Maya was so young, and that she had not experienced much of the war. And many saw her Asian features and remembered the enemy that the soldiers had died fighting against. They were mad that someone who looked like the Vietnamese would design the memorial. Maya may not have seen herself as Asian, but the rest of the world did.

People protested Maya's design. They called her horrible, racist names. At the government meeting to approve the memorial, people spoke angrily about her design. Maya had purposely made a design that was not about the government and its decisions, but she could not escape the arguments that happened in the government as a result. Some saw the V shape of the walls as a symbol for the letter V for victory. Others saw the shape as a nod to the anti-war protesters who often held up two fingers as a peace sign. Her design reminded everyone of the disagreements surrounding the war.

But Maya believed in her design. More than once, she faced a room full of angry men and defended her work. She even went on TV and talked to newspapers to explain her point of view.

Maya had to struggle for control of her design. Some wanted the names to be in alphabetical order instead of the order in which the soldiers had been

killed. But Maya argued that her order showed the history of the war. She also pointed out how many Smiths—a very common name—would be listed. Having a long list of Smiths would make the wall seem like a phone book. The critics realized Maya was right. They agreed to leave the names how Maya had designed them.

But for many protestors, it wasn't just about the details. They disliked the entire thing, and they wanted a completely different design. Secretary of the Interior James Watt, who was part of President Reagan's administration, was in charge of the memorial site. He refused to allow anything to be built unless changes were made. The Vietnam Veterans Memorial Fund searched for a compromise.

In the end, they decided to add a sculpture of three soldiers and a flagpole with an American flag to Maya's design. This satisfied the opponents, but Maya was outraged. It would distract from what her design was trying to do, and she felt that adding a statue by another artist was like "drawing moustaches on other peoples' portraits."

However, this was not a battle Maya could win. The Vietnam Veterans Memorial Fund could not have her memorial built without the additional statue. Their founder, Jan Scruggs, told Maya that the government had made its decision. Her only comfort was that the statue and flag would be put off to the side to keep the two memorials as separate as possible.

Even though many veterans hadn't understood her design on paper, Maya believed that "once it was up, they would get it." And she was right.

On November 13, 1982—a couple of days after Veterans Day—the Vietnam Veterans Memorial was dedicated. Years before, when the Vietnam veterans had first returned home, many had been treated badly, because there had been so much anger about the war itself. This dedication was to be the welcome home they had not been given. It was an elaborate five-day ceremony, and thousands of veterans and their loved ones came from all over the country.

When they saw the wall, they stared. It was as if they had come to a sacred place. They could not help touching the stone. Their fingers searched for the names of their friends, their brothers, their sons, their uncles, their fathers. People laid paper over the engraved names and rubbed pencils on them so they could capture an impression of the letters. Some placed flowers or notes at the base of the wall, or left offerings like shoes and hats. Many wept openly. Friends and family clutched each other.

Almost immediately, people forgot that they had been angry about Maya's design. Instead the memorial became, as the *New York Times* said, "a place for reverence, for homage, for silent tears."

To this day it gets around four million visitors a year. It has become a public sculpture that everyone treasures.

In the end, the wall helped heal the country. Maya had not meant for the memorial to be cheerful or happy, she had meant it to help people handle their sadness. And it did. The wall gently made everyone see the pain of the war. And only after that pain was accepted could people move forward.

······························

CHAPTER 6

After the Wall

Even though the Vietnam Veterans Memorial was a tremendous achievement, the struggle had left Maya feeling discouraged. While the wall was still being built, she decided to return to school for her master's degree. "I needed a place to start over," Maya said. First she went to Harvard University in Cambridge, Massachusetts. But trying to work in Washington and fit in at Harvard at the same time made Maya unhappy. She decided to return to familiar Yale. "Yale was like going home," Maya said.

She used this time to explore. Even though she was studying architecture, she found herself spending more time in the sculpture department. She loved creating art. Most professors wanted her to choose between sculpture and architecture, to specialize in one or the other. But Maya persisted. She knew she could do both.

Maya was also starting to see how being Asian American affected her. People had said the wall had an Asian influence. At first, Maya had felt that people only thought that because she had an Asian heritage. She did not think that her race and heritage were related to her work.

But many things had changed since her child-hood, when China had been mostly closed off to the United States. Now China and the United States were on friendlier terms, and Maya was able to visit with her family. When Maya saw her father's childhood house, which was simple and elegant and used natural materials that were common in Asian cultures, she began to understand. Those traits had been in her father's art, and now they had become a part of her work too.

Continuing to design and create helped her understand this even more. In 1988, Maya began work on a new project in Montgomery, Alabama. The Southern Poverty Law Center wanted her to design a civil rights memorial, one that would help visitors remember the Black people who had fought and sacrificed for equality in the US.

For this memorial, Maya inscribed a quote spoken by Martin Luther King Jr. on a curved black granite wall. In front of the wall, she placed a twelve-foot-wide round disk, which almost looked like a table. On it, she had carved a curving, unfinished timeline of the civil rights movement. Then she had water continually flow on both the wall and the table. Maya said that the water table was inspired by "Japanese water stones."

When the Civil Rights Memorial was

dedicated in 1989, people came to see it and touched the carved words. Their fingers made the water ripple. Their tears fell onto the table and became part of the running water. People became a part of the memorial. They joined the past and the present—just as Maya had intended.

This was only one of the many inspiring works Maya created after the Vietnam Veterans Memorial. She designed *Topo*, which used ball-shaped holly bushes to make the entrance to the Charlotte Coliseum look like a game for giants. For a project called *Wave Field*, she reshaped the land that surrounded an aerospace engineering building by echoing the work of the engineers and creating a series of sculpted waves in the earth. In *Groundswell*, she used broken glass to create her interpretation of a "swale in the ocean"—a low, shallow depression much like the streams that made the ridges in her backyard as a child.

For another project, the Langston Hughes Library, Maya transformed an old barn using glass and skylights so people would "always be connected to the land." The Juniata College Peace Chapel was an outdoor chapel consisting of a circle of stones for people to enjoy in the open air under the sky. The Riggio-Lynch Chapel was a wooden ark-like building with a ceiling that curved with arched beams. She also created a sculpture to commemorate women at Yale, designed the Museum of Chinese in America, and worked on a reading garden and private homes.

Maya's projects were all very different, but no matter what she designed, Maya considered the surrounding environment. Her childhood love of nature always impacted her work. "All my art-works deal with nature and the landscape," Maya said. "I do not believe anything I can create can compare to the beauty of the natural world, but these works are a response to that beauty."

Maya continues to create today. In 2009, she began work on what she called her last memorial, one intended to make people aware of endangered animals and problems facing the environment. Maya never became a field zoologist, but she never lost her love of animals.

Houses, museums, sculptures, gardens, art installations—Maya has designed all of them. Sometimes people are confused. Is Maya an artist or an architect?

Perhaps the label isn't important. No matter what she makes or what people think she is, each work is thoughtful. In each of the projects she's created, Maya wrote, "I recognize a distinctly Asian influence." She now fully accepts the influence of her heritage.

She has received many awards, including the National Medal of the Arts and even the Presidential Medal of Freedom! Those awards, presented by the president of the United States, are only given to people who have made extraordinary contributions to the country.

Along the way, Maya did more than work. In 1996, she married Daniel Wolf, a photography dealer. The couple had two daughters, India and Rachel. Having children was one reason why Maya truly accepted being Asian American. "I want my two children to know," Maya said about her Chinese heritage. "And I want to finally know it."

But Maya also knows that being Asian American is complicated. She can remember the many times strangers have asked her, "Where are you from?" When Maya answered that she was from Ohio, the strangers would become impatient or confused. They wanted to know what ethnicity she was, but, as she said, "It used to upset me to always be seen as *other*—not really from here . . . not really American."

This struggle shaped Maya's life and work. It made her feel like an observer, someone who watches. But being an observer helped her create work that fits in its environment. It helped her design memorials that heal people. It helped her show people what was missing.

So, is Maya Asian or American? Is she an artist or an architect?

Maya did not have to choose. Through her work and her family, she realized that she lives on the boundary of both. Asian, American, artist, architect—she is none of them, yet she is all of them. She is Maya Lin.

HOW YOU CAN PERSIST

by Grace Lin

I f you want to be an architect, an artist, or an advocate for the environment like Maya Lin, here are some things you can do:

1. Think about the subjects you enjoy learning about in school. Is there something you want to learn more about? Ask your teacher, parent, or another trusted adult if you can do some independent study and research

the topic further. You might even get extra credit!

2. Is there a place near your home where you can be in nature? It could be a park, a nearby woods, or even your backyard. Spend some time there and look at all the nature. Maybe bring a notebook and write (or draw) all the things you see. Pay attention to the details—the colors, sounds, and shapes. You might be surprised!

3. Find a way to make something! Look around and see what materials are nearby. Plastic bags? Empty boxes? Eggshells? Can you make something out of those things? What ideas do they give you?

4. Explore Maya's work! If you go to MayaLinStudio.com, you will see listings with photos of her art, architecture, and more. Spend some time looking through the links. Are any of her buildings, public art sculptures, exhibits, or installations near you? If so, see if you can plan a trip with your guardians to see it in person! Notice how different Maya's work looks in person compared to seeing it in photos. What are some differences you see?

5. Maya's "last memorial" (as she called it) is a series of public projects to bring awareness to climate change. Part of this series is a website called "What

Is Missing?" at WhatIsMissing.org.
Go to the website and learn about
the animals and ecosystems that are
disappearing. Try to see if an adult
will look though the site with you.
Even if they cannot, talk to the adults
in your life and see if they have seen
anything in the natural world that has
diminished or even disappeared. If they
have, consider "Sharing a Memory"
on the WhatIsMissing.org site. Then,
brainstorm ways you could help the
environment now.

6. Ask your parent or a trusted adult
   about your heritage and whether they
   have any history to share with you. If
   they don't, ask your teacher or librarian

to help you find books about the culture
you came from. Learn about your
heritage and think about how it could
affect what you do now.

7. Are there any contests that you would
enjoy entering? Ask your teacher or
librarian if they know of any. It could
be making a book, performing in a
talent show, or submitting something to
a baking contest. Do *not* worry about
winning or losing! To persist like Maya,
you just need to try!

ACKNOWLEDGMENTS

....

Special thanks to the Persisterhood publishing team who answered the call to add Asian American women to this outstanding series. I hope that I have done Maya Lin and all Asian American girls proud with this book. Much appreciation to the editors, copyeditors, and fact-checkers, who made sure this book remained nonfiction, specifically: Jill Santopolo, Talia Benamy, Shara Hardeson, and Krista Ahlberg.

❧ References ❧

BOOKS:

Harvey, Jeanne Walker. *Maya Lin: Artist-Architect of Light and Lines*. New York: Henry Holt and Company, 2017.

Lashnits, Tom. *Maya Lin*. New York: Chelsea House, 2007.

Lin, Maya. *Boundaries*. New York: Simon & Schuster, 2000.

Lin, Maya Ying. *Maya Lin: Systematic Landscapes*. Essays by Richard Andrews, John

Beardsley; foreword by Lawrence Weschler. New Haven: Yale University Press, 2006.

Lin, Maya Ying. *Maya Lin: Topologies*. Essays by Michael Brenson, William L. Fox, Paul Goldberger; foreword by John McPhee. New York: Rizzoli, 2015.

Malone, Mary. *Maya Lin: Architect and Artist*. Springfield, NJ: Enslow Publishers, 1995.

Rubin, Susan Goldman. *Maya Lin: Thinking with Her Hands*. San Francisco: Chronicle Books, 2017.

DOCUMENTARY:

Mock, Freida Lee. *Maya Lin: A Strong Clear Vision*. 1994; United States: Docurama, 2003. DVD.

INTERNET SOURCES:

Academy of Achievement. "Maya Lin —
Academy of Achievement." Last modified
February 7, 2022. Accessed March 2021.
achievement.org/achiever/maya-lin
/#profile.

"Julia Lin," obituary. *The Athens Messenger*,
August 23, 2013. athensmessenger.com
/obituaries/julia-lin/article_436f09b3-2511
-5530-bd46-4f14bf43d447.html.

Lin, Maya. "A Conversation with Maya Lin."
Interview by Bill Moyers. "Moyer's Moments,"
NPR, April 25, 2003. billmoyers.com/content
/maya-lin-extended.

Morgan, William. "Muted but Monumental: The Vietnam Veterans Memorial." AIA. Accessed March 2021. aia.org/articles/6143509-muted -but-monumental-the-vietnam-veterans-:16.

Sokol, Brett. "For Maya Lin, a Victory Lap Gives Way to Mourning." *The New York Times*, March 17, 2021. nytimes.com/2021/03/17/arts /design/maya-lin-smith-college-daniel-wolf.html.

Waddoups, Ryan. "The Deeply Personal Story Behind Maya Lin's Latest Project." *Surface* magazine, March 23, 2021. surfacemag.com /articles/maya-lin-neilson-library-smith-college.

GRACE LIN is the *New York Times* bestselling and award-winning author/illustrator of *Where the Mountain Meets the Moon, Ling & Ting, When the Sea Turned to Silver,* and *A Big Mooncake for Little Star.* Grace is also a commentator for New England Public Radio, a video essayist for *PBS NewsHour,* and the speaker of the popular TEDx Talk "The Windows and Mirrors of Your Child's Bookshelf," as well as the host of two podcasts: *Book Friends Forever* and *Kids Ask Authors.* In 2016, Grace's art was displayed at the White House, where Grace herself was recognized by President Obama's office as a Champion of Change for Asian American and Pacific Islander Art and Storytelling, and in 2022, Grace was the recipient of the Children's Literature Legacy Award from the American Library Association.

You can visit Grace online at
gracelin.com
and follow her on Twitter and Instagram
@pacylin

GILLIAN FLINT has worked as a professional illustrator since earning an animation and illustration degree in 2003. Her work has since been published in the UK, USA and Australia. In her spare time, Gillian enjoys reading, spending time with her family and puttering about in the garden on sunny days. She lives in the northwest of England.

You can visit Gillian Flint online at
gillianflint.com
or follow her on Twitter
@GillianFlint
and on Instagram
@gillianflint_illustration

CHELSEA CLINTON is the author of the #1 *New York Times* bestseller *She Persisted: 13 American Women Who Changed the World*; *She Persisted Around the World: 13 Women Who Changed History*; *She Persisted in Sports: American Olympians Who Changed the Game*; *Don't Let Them Disappear: 12 Endangered Species Across the Globe*; *It's Your World: Get Informed, Get Inspired & Get Going!*; *Start Now!: You Can Make a Difference*; with Hillary Clinton, *Grandma's Gardens* and *The Book of Gutsy Women*; and, with Devi Sridhar, *Governing Global Health: Who Runs the World and Why?* She is also the Vice Chair of the Clinton Foundation, where she works on many initiatives, including those that help empower the next generation of leaders. She lives in New York City with her husband, Marc, their children and their dog, Soren.

You can follow Chelsea Clinton on Twitter
@ChelseaClinton
or on Facebook at
facebook.com/chelseaclinton

ALEXANDRA BOIGER has illustrated nearly twenty picture books, including the She Persisted books by Chelsea Clinton; the popular Tallulah series by Marilyn Singer; and the Max and Marla books, which she also wrote. Originally from Munich, Germany, she now lives outside of San Francisco, California, with her husband, Andrea, daughter, Vanessa, and two cats, Luiso and Winter.

You can visit Alexandra Boiger online at
alexandraboiger.com
or follow her on Instagram
@alexandra_boiger

Read about more inspiring women in the

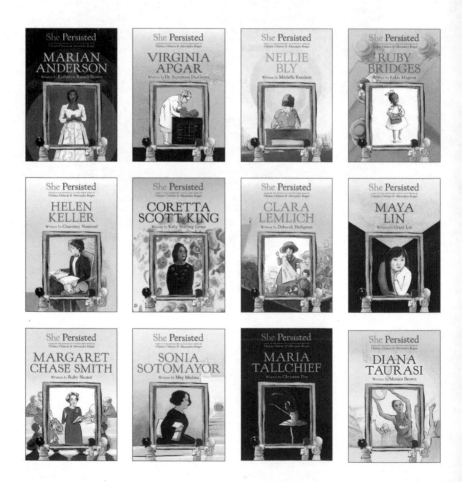